I0423785

Contents

Summary

The unemployment insurance (UI) system is a partnership between the federal government and state governments that provides a temporary weekly benefit to qualified workers who lose their job and are seeking work. The amount of that benefit is based in part on a worker's past earnings. The Congressional Budget Office (CBO) estimates that UI benefits totaled $94 billion in fiscal year 2012 (when the unemployment rate was 8.3 percent, on average), a substantial increase over the $33 billion paid out in fiscal year 2007 (when the unemployment rate was 4.5 percent, on average).

The periods for which eligible workers can receive UI benefits have been repeatedly extended during the recent recession and its aftermath. Regular UI benefits generally last up to 26 weeks (see Summary Table 1). Additional weeks of benefits have been provided through the creation of the temporary Emergency Unemployment Compensation (EUC) program in 2008 and through modifications to the extended benefits (EB) program. The EUC program currently provides up to 47 weeks of additional benefits (depending on a state's unemployment rate) after regular UI benefits have been exhausted. The EB program provides up to 20 weeks of benefits to certain eligible workers who have exhausted their EUC benefits (temporary changes in law have made it easier for states to qualify to provide extended benefits and have made the funding for the EB program entirely federal). The benefits the three programs provide—at a total cost over the past five years of roughly $520 billion—have allowed households to better maintain their consumption while household members are unemployed. Under current law, the temporary benefits that have been provided in recent years are set to expire at the end of December 2012.

CBO assessed four options that would extend some or all of the current benefits for up to one year and estimated their costs to the federal budget (shown in parentheses), as follows:

- **Option 1:** Fully extend the current EUC program and temporary provisions of the EB program for one year ($30 billion);

- **Option 2:** Partially extend the current EUC program by providing at most 14 extra weeks of benefits for one year ($14 billion);

- **Option 3:** Allow UI recipients to finish receiving up to 14 weeks of EUC benefits, depending on the number of weeks of benefits for which they will qualify at the end of December 2012 ($4 billion); and

- **Option 4:** Extend the current EB program for one year, maintaining full federal funding and allowing states to more easily qualify for the program ($3 billion).

Those options to extend UI benefits would have several effects on individuals and the U.S. economy in the short run. In particular, they would:

- Afford greater protection against income lost during unemployment;

- Provide incentives for UI recipients to remain unemployed longer than they otherwise would have because UI benefits stop when recipients find a job or stop looking for work; and

- Lead to more consumer spending and increased demand for goods and services, which CBO expects would boost overall output and employment in the short term.

The four options would have similar short-term macroeconomic effects per dollar of budgetary cost. (Option 3

Summary Table 1.

Unemployment Insurance Programs in Effect as of December 1, 2012

Program	Enabling Legislation	Funding	Eligibility	Weekly Benefits	
				Maximum Weeks Available	Amount
Regular Unemployment Insurance	Social Security Act of 1935	A state UI payroll tax on employers pays for benefits, and a federal UI payroll tax on employers pays for states' administrative expenses.	Workers must have lost their job through no fault of their own (typically, because they were laid off) and must have had a consistent record of earnings during a base period (typically, the previous four or five quarters).	26 weeks in most states; as few as 19 weeks in others.	Amounts vary, but weekly benefits are typically about 50 percent of prior weekly earnings up to a state-specific cap. In 2009, the average weekly benefit was $300.
Emergency Unemployment Compensation	Enacted in the Supplemental Appropriations Act, 2008; modified by subsequent acts, most recently by the Middle Class Tax Relief and Job Creation Act of 2012	Fully funded by the federal government from general revenues.	Workers' eligibility is the same as for regular UI benefits. States qualify if their unemployment rate meets certain criteria.	14 to 47 weeks of benefits are currently offered, depending on the state's unemployment rate, but the number of weeks offered since 2009 has been as high as 53.	Same as regular UI benefits.
Extended Benefits	Federal-State Extended Unemployment Compensation Act of 1970	Normally funded 50/50 by states and the federal government but currently funded fully by the federal government.	Workers' eligibility is typically the same as for regular UI benefits. States qualify if their unemployment rate is high and increasing.	0, 13, or 20 weeks of benefits, depending on the state's unemployment rate.	Same as regular UI benefits.

Source: Congressional Budget Office.

Note: UI = unemployment insurance.

would have slightly larger economic effects per dollar of budgetary cost in 2013 because spending would be concentrated earlier in the year; but that option would have the same cumulative effects over several years.) For the three options involving extensions for an entire year—Options 1, 2, and 4—economic output would be $1.10 higher per dollar of budgetary cost, on average, in 2013, CBO estimates, and employment would be increased by six years of full-time equivalent employment per million dollars of budgetary cost (see Summary Figure 1). Under Option 1, for example, which extends the benefits provided under the current EUC and EB programs at a total budgetary cost of $30 billion, CBO estimates that gross domestic product adjusted for inflation would be 0.2 percent higher in the fourth

quarter of 2013 and that full-time-equivalent employment would be 0.3 million higher at that time than it would be under current law. (The overall effects for the fourth quarter of 2013 are not equal to the corresponding effects per dollar multiplied by the budgetary cost reported above because of differences in the time periods analyzed.)

CBO also considered a fifth option that would provide temporary fiscal relief to states by delaying for one year the repayment of funds they have borrowed from the Unemployment Trust Fund, which is funded by a federal payroll tax on employers. Under Option 5, the federal government would forgo about $3 billion of revenue in

Summary Figure 1.

Estimated Economic Effects in 2013 of Extending Unemployment Benefits, Relative to the Budgetary Cost in 2013

Gross Domestic Product
(Dollars of GDP in 2013 per dollar
of budgetary cost in 2013)

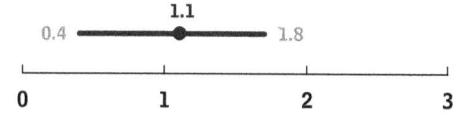

**Extend Unemployment Insurance
Benefits for One Year**[a]

Full-Time-Equivalent Employment Years
(Average in 2013 per million dollars
of budgetary cost in 2013)

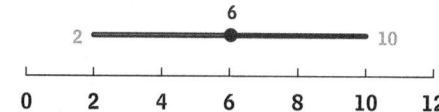

Source: Congressional Budget Office.

Notes: The dots represent CBO's central estimates, which correspond to the assumption that the values that describe key parameters of economic behavior (in particular, the extent to which lower federal taxes and higher federal spending boost aggregate demand in the short term) equal the midpoints of the ranges used by CBO. The ends of the lines represent estimates based on the full ranges that CBO uses for those parameters.

The estimated budgetary cost does not include debt service.

a.   The results shown here apply to fully extending the Emergency Unemployment Compensation (EUC) program and temporary provisions of the extended benefits (EB) program for one year (Option 1), partially extending the EUC program for one year (Option 2), or extending temporary provisions of the EB program for one year (Option 4). The economic effects relative to the budgetary cost would be slightly larger if recipients of unemployment insurance were allowed to finish receiving up to 14 additional weeks of the EUC benefits for which they will qualify at the end of December 2012 (Option 3) because that spending would be concentrated earlier in the year.

2013 but would collect roughly that same amount in subsequent years.

In addition, CBO assessed more fundamental modifications of the UI system over the longer term. Some of those approaches would promote employment by increasing incentives for UI recipients to take a new job or by encouraging firms to reduce hours worked per employee rather than lay off some workers while retaining others full time. Other approaches would change the federal and state roles in administering UI, either by making the amount of funding more predictable and giving states more flexibility in implementing their UI programs or by making UI benefits and tax rates more uniform among states. Still other approaches would alter the distribution of resources within the UI system by expanding the wage base on which UI taxes are levied, by changing the weekly benefits the system provides, or by providing insurance against the earnings loss that many laid-off workers experience when they take a new job.

Unemployment Insurance in the Wake of the Recent Recession

The Unemployment Insurance System

The unemployment insurance (UI) system is a partnership between the federal government and the states that provides payments to eligible workers who have been laid off. States vary considerably in their rules governing eligibility for benefits, benefit amounts, and payroll tax rates. Employers pay a state payroll tax to fund some of those benefits. Each state has its own account in the Unemployment Trust Fund (referred to in this report as the UI trust fund). When a state's unemployment rate is high and its benefit payments exceed its payroll tax revenues, the state can draw from its account in the trust fund to cover the benefit payments. Employers also pay a federal payroll tax that is deposited into federal accounts in the trust fund. Those accounts are tapped for state and federal administrative costs, the federal share of certain benefits, and advances to states that cannot pay their regular benefits in a timely way.

UI benefits expanded considerably during and after the recent recession. The unemployment rate rose from about 5 percent in 2007 to nearly 10 percent in the latter months of 2009, and the share of unemployed people who had not worked for 26 weeks or more increased substantially. In response, policymakers changed the UI system in several ways: They increased the number of weeks for which workers can receive benefits, increased the amount of benefits, and shifted more of the responsibility for funding UI programs to the federal government. As a result, UI benefits peaked at more than $150 billion during 2010 (when the annual unemployment rate peaked at 9.6 percent). Unemployment and benefit payments have both declined since then.

The UI system currently comprises three programs that provide benefits to unemployed workers:

- The regular UI program, which was enacted in the Social Security Act of 1935;

- The Emergency Unemployment Compensation (EUC) program, which went into effect in July 2008 and provides benefits to unemployed workers who have exhausted their regular UI benefits; and

- The extended benefits (EB) program, which has been in effect since 1970 and, under certain circumstances, provides benefits once the regular and EUC benefits have been exhausted. In the absence of the EUC program, people who have exhausted their regular benefits receive additional assistance through the EB program if they reside in qualifying states.

Benefits Under the Regular UI Program

The regular UI program is administered by the states. It provides payments to people who apply for benefits and are deemed eligible to receive them because they have been laid off or because they have left the military (at the end of their contract period or for health reasons). People who quit their job or are fired are generally not eligible for UI benefits, nor are people who are entering or reentering the labor market. To be eligible for benefits, workers must have earned at least a certain amount of income in the recent past, typically for four of the five most recent quarters; the amount of income varies by state. Thus, for example, new college graduates without a job do not typically receive UI benefits. To maintain eligibility for benefits while unemployed, UI recipients must search for a new job and, in some states, must accept a reasonable job offer.[1]

---

1. For more details, see Christopher J. O'Leary, "State UI Job Search Rules and Reemployment Services," *Monthly Labor Review*, vol. 129, no. 6 (June 2006), pp. 27–37, www.bls.gov/opub/mlr/2006/06/art3full.pdf.

Recipients can generally receive up to 26 weeks of benefits under the regular UI program, although as of October 1, 2012, seven states had shorter limits. The amount of weekly UI benefits depends on an individual's prior earnings; higher earners receive higher benefits, up to a maximum benefit. Average weekly UI benefits vary from state to state because of differences in average earnings and benefit formulas. Nationwide average UI benefits, which change from year to year because of variability in recipients' earnings history and state of residence, have been about $300 per week since 2009. The weekly amount a worker receives usually does not change during the period that he or she collects unemployment insurance benefits.

The ratio of UI benefits to prior cash earnings—termed the UI replacement rate—varies from state to state and from person to person. In general, UI replacement rates range from 30 percent to 50 percent of prior earnings, and workers with higher earnings are at the lower end of that range because of the cap on weekly benefits.

Additional Benefits During the Past Five Years

The number of people receiving UI benefits rose during and after the recent recession for several reasons. Far more workers were laid off in 2008 and 2009 than in 2006 and 2007. Having so many more workers eligible for unemployment benefits would have substantially increased the number of recipients in the absence of any change in UI policies, but federal policies also were changed in ways that further expanded the number of UI recipients. The most important change increased the number of weeks for which laid-off workers could receive emergency and extended benefits; other changes also temporarily raised the amount of those weekly benefits. Together, those changes increased the share of unemployed workers who were eligible for benefits and, by making the benefits more attractive, increased the share who chose to receive them.[2] The changes in the UI system were made through several specific programs.

Emergency Unemployment Compensation. The EUC program, which is funded entirely by the federal government, has provided additional weeks of UI benefits to eligible unemployed workers since July 2008. Benefits in the EUC program are in four tiers. Workers in every state currently qualify for 14 weeks of emergency benefits (the first tier). Eligibility for three higher tiers—each providing between 9 and 14 additional weeks of benefits—has been limited to unemployed workers in states with higher unemployment rates and has changed over time.[3]

Extended Benefits. The EB program was established in 1970 and currently provides either 13 or 20 weeks of additional benefits to unemployed workers in certain states who have exhausted their regular and emergency benefits. Benefits are normally available in states whose insured unemployment rate (the ratio of the number of UI benefit recipients to the number of workers covered by the system) is higher than 5 percent and is also at least 20 percent higher than it had been in both of the previous two years. States have the option to choose a higher trigger—6 percent—without the requirement that the rate be rising. In addition, states have the option of basing their eligibility for extended benefits on their standard unemployment rate (the ratio of the number of people who are unemployed to the number in the workforce). Using that option, states can qualify for 13 weeks of extended benefits if their unemployment rate is both rising and exceeds a threshold, and they may qualify for 20 weeks if their unemployment rate is rising and exceeds a higher threshold.

Provisions in the Tax Relief, Unemployment Insurance Reauthorization, and Job Creation Act of 2010 made it easier for states to reach the thresholds, or "triggers," for eligibility for extended benefits. That law allows states to adopt a three-year "look-back" period with which current unemployment is compared in determining whether a state's unemployment rate is rising; the previous look-back period was two years. In essence, the extended look-back provision allows states to compare their unemployment rate with the corresponding rates in earlier years (when unemployment rates were generally low) rather than with the rates in 2010 or 2011 (when unemployment rates were generally higher than they are

2. For a discussion of the factors underlying a decision to accept UI benefits during earlier periods, see Rebecca M. Blank and David E. Card, "Recent Trends in Insured and Uninsured Unemployment: Is There an Explanation?" *Quarterly Journal of Economics*, vol. 106, no. 4 (November 1991), pp. 1157–1189, http://qje.oxfordjournals.org/content/106/4/1157.abstract; and Patricia M. Anderson and Bruce D. Meyer, "Unemployment Insurance Takeup Rates and the After-Tax Value of Benefits," *Quarterly Journal of Economics*, vol. 112, no. 3 (August 1997), pp. 913–937, http://qje.oxfordjournals.org/content/112/3/913.abstract.

3. For more information about the EUC program in 2012, see Department of Labor, *Emergency Unemployment Compensation 2008 (EUC) Program* (February 27, 2012), www.workforcesecurity.doleta.gov/unemploy/pdf/euc08.pdf.

today). As a result, more states have been eligible to provide extended benefits over the past five years, although New York was the only eligible state as of November 2012.

Maximum Duration of Benefits. The collective provision of regular benefits (up to 26 weeks), emergency benefits (at their height, up to 53 weeks), and extended benefits (up to 20 weeks) means that a person who was laid off during the past few years could have received benefits for up to 99 weeks, although in many states and at various times the maximum has been much lower.

Other Changes. In addition to extending the duration of benefits, the federal government temporarily increased the amount of the weekly benefit by $25 (referred to as federal additional compensation) between February 2009 and early June 2010. It also changed the tax treatment of unemployment benefits. For tax year 2009 only, UI recipients could exclude from federal income taxation the first $2,400 of UI benefits they received. That exclusion was worth $360 in after-tax dollars for the typical recipient, who was in the 15 percent tax bracket.

Funding for Unemployment Insurance

Funding for unemployment insurance is ordinarily drawn from payroll taxes imposed on employers by state governments and the federal government. All funds collected through UI payroll taxes are deposited in the UI trust fund and appear as part of the federal budget. The trust fund allows states to save during good times, to draw down their account with the trust fund when their UI expenditures exceed tax receipts, and to borrow when they have insufficient balances to cover UI benefits. In recent years, funding for portions of the unemployment insurance program, such as emergency benefits, have been paid for out of general federal revenues rather than from dedicated payroll taxes.

State Payroll Taxes. The amount of state payroll taxes an employer pays for any particular employee is the product of the firm's state UI tax rate and the amount of the worker's earnings subject to the UI tax in that state. State UI tax rates vary among employers; higher rates are levied on employers with a history of costly UI claims. (The process by which states adjust employers' UI tax rates in response to historical UI claims is called "experience rating.") All states have minimum and maximum tax rates that apply to employers. In July 2012, minimum tax rates ranged from zero percent (in several states) to

2.6 percent (in New Hampshire), and maximum rates ranged from 5.4 percent (in many states) to 13.5 percent (in Maryland).

State UI taxes are levied as a percentage of each employee's earnings, up to a maximum taxable wage base (that is, the amount of earnings subject to the UI tax). In 2012, for example, those wage bases ranged from $7,000 in Arizona and California to $38,800 in Hawaii. The limit on taxable wages for any worker means that UI taxes account for a higher percentage of earnings for workers with low earnings than for those with high earnings. In the Congressional Budget Office's (CBO's) view, the portion of UI taxes that does not vary among firms within a local labor market is generally passed through to workers in the form of reduced earnings; under that view, the reduced earnings resulting from the payroll tax accounts for a larger share of earnings for low earners than for high earners.[4] Low earners, however, also tend to receive larger benefits as a share of earnings than do high earners.[5]

Federal Payroll Taxes. The Federal Unemployment Tax Act (FUTA) imposes a payroll tax on employers to pay states' UI administrative costs and the federal share of the EB program and to provide the trust fund from which states can draw advances (to be repaid with interest) if their UI accounts are fully depleted. The FUTA tax rate is 6.0 percent on the first $7,000 paid to each employee, but almost all employers receive a credit of 5.4 percent for state taxes paid. The net effect is therefore a tax of 0.6 percent, or a maximum of $42, on employees earning at least $7,000 annually. Beginning in 1976, a FUTA surtax of 0.2 percent brought the total FUTA tax, net of the state tax credits, to 0.8 percent (for a maximum of $56 per employee), but those surtax provisions expired on July 1, 2011.

---

4. One study finds that individual firms can pass through only a small share of the differences between firms within a local labor market that are attributable to experience rating. See Patricia M. Anderson and Bruce D. Meyer, "The Effects of Firm Specific Taxes and Government Mandates with an Application to the U.S. Unemployment Insurance Program," *Journal of Public Economics*, vol. 65, no. 2 (August 1997), pp. 119–145, www.sciencedirect.com/science/journal/00472727/65/2.

5. Patricia M. Anderson and Bruce D. Meyer, "Unemployment Insurance Tax Burdens and Benefits: Funding Family Leave and Reforming the Payroll Tax," *National Tax Journal*, vol. 59, no. 1 (March 2006), pp. 77–95, http://ntanet.org/tax-resources/ntj-full-text-articles.html.

States can pay off advances from the trust fund if their UI tax receipts exceed the amount of UI benefits they pay out. That can occur if states raise their UI taxable wage bases or their UI tax rates, or if their economies improve, in which case UI tax receipts naturally rise and UI expenditures naturally fall. Alternatively, states can repay the trust fund with funds that they borrow by issuing bonds. If a state's balance is not paid off within a certain period, then the credit for state taxes paid is automatically reduced, causing its FUTA tax rate to rise to help reduce the balance. Specifically, under current law, states that are in debt to the UI trust fund and that do not adequately increase their payments have their FUTA tax rates automatically increased by 0.3 percentage points per year (or more) when that debt remains outstanding for two or more consecutive years.[6]

Funding for UI During the Past Five Years. State UI payroll taxes are typically adequate to cover UI expenditures when unemployment is low, but expenditures in many cases exceed UI taxes when unemployment is high. In 2007, before the recent recession began, the states collectively had a balance of roughly $40 billion in the trust fund. As of June 30, 2012, however, after several years of lower UI revenues and much higher UI expenditures, state loans from the trust fund (net of positive balances) totaled $13 billion.[7] To pay back that borrowing and to fund continuing high UI expenditures, some states have modified their UI tax systems to raise more revenue. (Some states have also reduced the number of weeks that benefits are available.) As a result, the nationwide ratio of state UI taxes collected to total earnings—the average state UI tax rate—has increased from about 0.6 percent in 2008 to 0.9 percent in 2012.

Some states have been unable to pay off their debt to the UI trust fund despite their increased tax rates and reduced benefits, and in some cases those states' FUTA tax rates have automatically increased. Indiana, for example, had a FUTA tax rate of 1.2 percent in 2011. As a result, Indiana employers paid a FUTA tax of $84 for each employee earning more than $7,000 per year (the

$42 they normally would have paid plus an extra $42 because of the state's indebtedness to the trust fund).

Funding arrangements are different for the extended benefits program and the Emergency Unemployment Compensation program. The EB program is usually funded in equal shares by the federal government and state governments but has been funded completely by the federal government since February 2009—initially pursuant to the American Recovery and Reinvestment Act of 2009 and most recently to the Middle Class Tax Relief and Job Creation Act of 2012. The EUC program has been funded entirely by the federal government and has been available since July 2008.[8] Although the federal government instituted programs similar to the EUC program during and after previous recessions, nothing in prior law required the provision of EUC benefits following the recent recession.

Recipients of UI Benefits and the Budgetary Cost of Benefits

Increased layoffs among workers and policy changes in the UI system have expanded the number of recipients and the amount spent to provide unemployment benefits. The unemployment rate increased during and after the recession, in part because so many workers were laid off but also because finding a new job took longer for unemployed workers (regardless of whether they had been laid off or were unemployed for some other reason). In addition, the proportion of unemployment accounted for by the long-term unemployed (that is, by people who have been unemployed for at least 26 weeks) steadily increased, reaching all-time highs in 2010 and 2011.[9] Many of those laid-off workers were eligible for unemployment benefits, and so spending in the UI system also increased in those years.

An average of roughly 8 million workers who lost their job started receiving UI benefits in each fiscal year from 2004 to 2007. That number grew substantially and peaked at 14.4 million in 2009 (see Figure 1). In addition to the increase in the number of new recipients, the

6. See Julie M. Whittaker, *The Unemployment Trust Fund (UTF): State Insolvency and Federal Loans to States*, CRS Report for Congress RS22954 (Congressional Research Service, September 20, 2012).

7. See Department of Labor, *Unemployment Insurance Data Summary* (2nd quarter 2012), p. 8, http://workforcesecurity.doleta.gov/ unemploy/content/data_stats/datasum12/DataSum_2012_2.pdf.

8. The Supplemental Appropriations Act of 2008 (Public Law 110-252) established the EUC program. The most recent extension of EUC benefits was in the Middle Class Tax Relief and Job Creation Act of 2012.

9. Congressional Budget Office, *Understanding and Responding to Persistently High Unemployment* (February 2012), www.cbo.gov/ publication/42989.

Figure 1.

Number of People Who Began Receiving Unemployment Benefits, by Fiscal Year

(Millions)

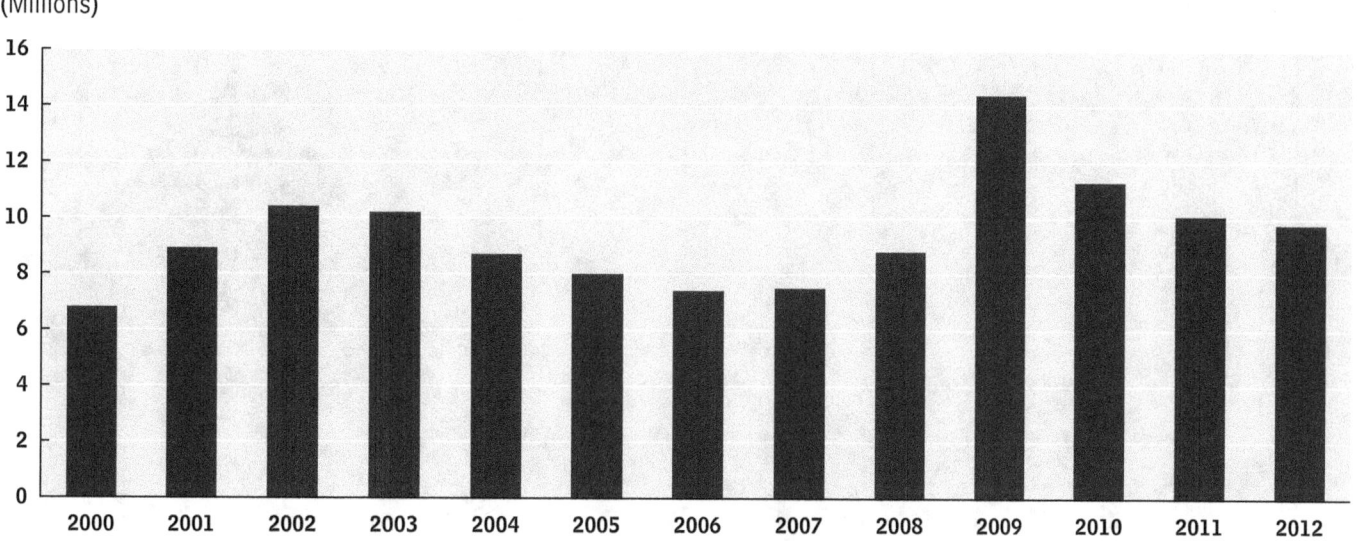

Source: Congressional Budget Office based on data from the Department of Labor, Employment and Training Administration.

total number of recipients each year also went up because unemployed workers received those benefits for longer periods. Eligible workers received benefits for longer periods both because finding work became more difficult and because they could receive UI benefits for an extended period. The share of UI recipients who exhausted their regular benefits, which in most states last for 26 weeks, increased from roughly 35 percent between 2004 and 2007 to 44 percent in 2009 and 62 percent in 2010.

Greater numbers of people receiving UI benefits and higher benefits per person have increased UI spending (see Figure 2). (Although taxes and benefits are largely set by individual states, all UI taxes and expenditures are recorded in the federal budget.) The unemployment rate and benefits both peaked in 2010 and have since fallen off, but the proportionate drop has been greater for benefits. In particular, since 2010, two factors have decreased the share of unemployed workers who are eligible for those benefits. First, since peaking in 2008 and 2009, the number of workers laid off has decreased, which means that the unemployed are increasingly people seeking their first job and those reentering the workforce—groups who are typically not eligible for UI benefits. Second, workers who were laid off in 2008 and 2009 have now exhausted their benefits—even if they were in a state in which they were eligible for the maximum 99 weeks of benefits.

Economic Effects of Unemployment Insurance

The unemployment insurance system—as it existed before 2008 and in its current form—affects the economy through several channels:

■ UI benefits insure workers against losses in income and provide them with cash to pay current expenses if they are laid off.

■ UI benefits increase incentives for workers who lose their job to look for work (by requiring them to do so in order to receive benefits) but reduce the incentives to accept a job offer.

■ UI taxes change employers' and recipients' decisions about employment.

■ The UI system serves as an automatic economic stabilizer by supporting consumer spending when income falls, which in turn boosts aggregate economic activity.

Effects of UI Benefits on Income, Consumption, and Saving

Insurance protects people from the consequences of certain events; in the case of unemployment insurance, it protects against some of the losses in earnings and consumption that might otherwise follow a layoff. Between

Figure 2.

Spending on Unemployment Benefits, by Fiscal Year

(Billions of dollars)

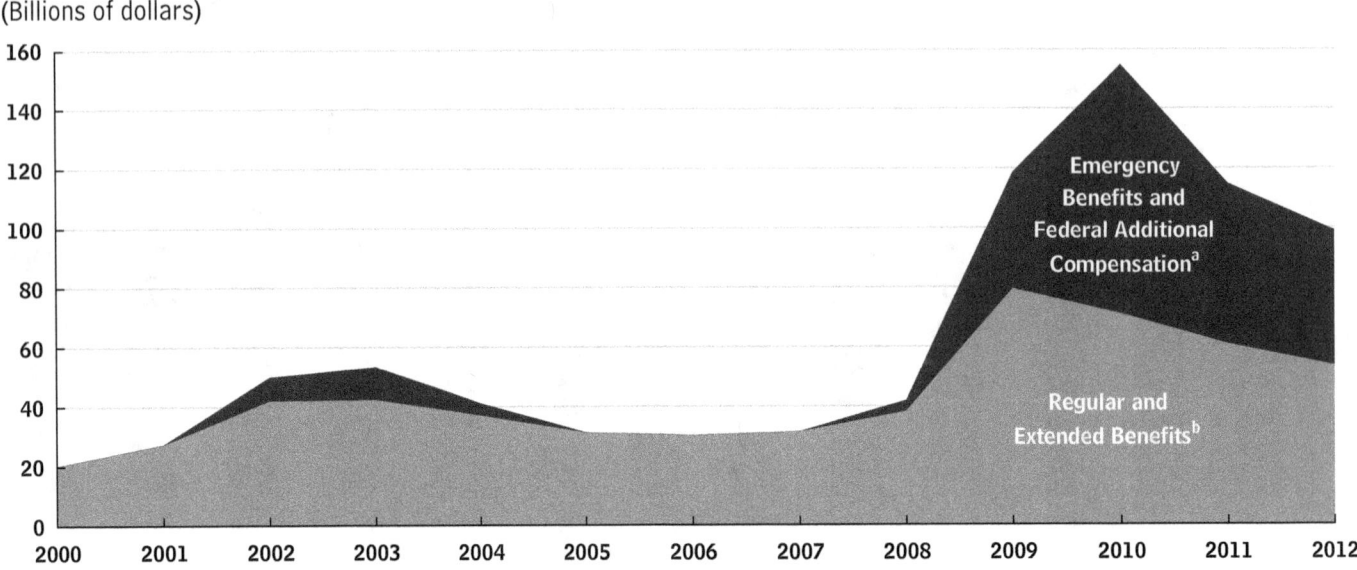

Source: Congressional Budget Office based on data from the Department of Labor, Employment and Training Administration.

a.   Emergency benefits may be temporarily authorized during periods of high unemployment, as they were from March 2002 through March 2004 and from July 2008 through December 2012. A weekly supplement of $25, termed federal additional compensation, was available to people receiving unemployment benefits between February 2009 and June 2010.

b.   Regular benefits are provided according to state laws under broad federal parameters. Typically, regular benefits are available for up to 26 weeks. Extended benefits may provide an additional 13 or 20 weeks of benefits, depending on a state's laws and unemployment rate.

fiscal years 2008 and 2012, the UI system provided $520 billion to unemployed people, using funds that were raised through UI payroll taxes and general revenues.

That insurance keeps some families from entering poverty when a family member loses a job. About 70 percent of UI benefits paid out in 2009 went to families whose income exceeded 200 percent of the federal poverty threshold because another family member had labor income or the family had other sources of income. But a substantial portion of benefits went to families who were below or near that threshold. For many of those families, UI benefits were the difference between being in or out of poverty. The poverty rate was 14.3 percent in 2009, for example, whereas without UI benefits (and assuming that other income sources would not have changed), it would have been 15.4 percent.[10]

Unemployment insurance allows some unemployed people to avoid having to raise cash by selling assets, such as cars, to pay for more immediate needs, such as food and housing. For workers who have a job, the availability of unemployment insurance enables them to hold less of their savings in liquid forms, such as checking accounts, and to hold more of their savings in less readily accessible forms, such as retirement accounts and certificates of deposit. Specifically, without that insurance, workers might worry about the penalties associated with accessing their illiquid savings if they became unemployed. By providing cash when it is needed, unemployment insurance allows households to keep more of their savings in forms that are harder to access quickly but that may offer better returns.[11]

Similarly, the availability of unemployment insurance enables workers to take more risks in their career. In the

---

10. Congressional Budget Office, *Unemployment Insurance Benefits and Family Income of the Unemployed* (November 2010), www.cbo.gov/publication/21922.

11. See Raj Chetty, "Moral Hazard Versus Liquidity and Optimal Unemployment Insurance," *Journal of Political Economy*, vol. 116, no. 2 (April 2008), pp. 173–234, www.jstor.org/stable/10.1086/529035.

absence of that insurance, workers might be overcautious and take a job that has less chance of a layoff but that also has less chance of a financial gain. For example, without UI, workers might be reluctant to take a job with a new, small firm that could either grow rapidly or fail. That insurance benefit for individuals may also help the overall economy. Some research suggests that the current UI system boosts productivity because it allows workers to take more risks that are socially efficient and that such an effect may more than compensate for the reduced efficiency that arises from the effects of UI on incentives to work.[12]

Effects of UI Benefits on Incentives to Search for Work and Accept a Job Offer

The structure of UI benefits increases the incentive for workers who lose their job to search for one, but it decreases their incentive to accept a job offer. Those changes in incentives differ during times of high unemployment.

Searching for a Job. The UI program requires that benefit recipients actively look for work; as a result, some laid-off workers who might otherwise have left the workforce (that is, neither worked nor sought work) may instead eventually return to work. That effect may be weak, however, because the financial penalties that the UI system imposes on recipients who do not actively search for work are inconsistently applied. One recent study found that recipients with higher weekly UI benefits searched much less actively than those with lower benefits, suggesting that more generous UI benefits discourage looking for a job.[13] Evidence of whether a more active job search leads to a better job is sparse, but a recent study of workers in Germany found that longer spells of receiving unemployment benefits slightly reduced workers' long-run earnings.[14]

Accepting a Job Offer. The UI system reduces the incentive for benefit recipients to accept a job offer because the earnings from that job will be partially offset by the

discontinuation of their UI benefits. For example, an unemployed worker who is currently receiving UI benefits and is considering accepting a job that would pay $600 per week (or about $30,000 per year) after taxes would lose those benefits if he or she took the job. If the worker received $300 per week after taxes from UI benefits, then taking the job would increase his or her income by only $300 per week after the loss of those benefits is taken into account. In this example, UI represents a 50 percent effective marginal tax rate on earnings, which reduces the financial benefit of taking a job as long as UI benefits are available. (That tax rate is lower for workers whose benefit amounts are low relative to the earnings they could receive from a new job.) The net effect is that unemployment insurance would be expected to increase the amount of time that recipients remain unemployed.

Indeed, empirical studies have found that UI affects the rate at which recipients accept new jobs. For example, research has shown that many workers find jobs in the weeks immediately before and after their benefits run out. Studies of the duration of unemployment in periods during which states changed the structure of their UI systems—say, by increasing benefit amounts or by allowing more weeks of benefit receipt—reported similar conclusions.[15] One widely cited study from 1990 found that eligibility for five extra weeks of benefits led, on average, to a one-week increase in the length of an unemployment spell.[16] A more recent study suggested, however, that

12. See Daron Acemoglu and Robert Shimer, "Productivity Gains from Unemployment Insurance," *European Economic Review*, vol. 44, no. 7 (June 2000), pp. 1195–1224, www.sciencedirect.com/science/article/pii/S0014292100000350.

13. See Alan B. Krueger and Andreas Mueller, "Job Search and Unemployment Insurance: New Evidence from Time Use Data," *Journal of Public Economics*, vol. 94, nos. 3–4 (April 2010), pp. 298–307, www.sciencedirect.com/science/journal/00472727/94/3-4.

14. See Johannes F. Schmieder, Till von Wachter, and Stefan Bender, "The Effects of Unemployment Insurance on Labor Supply and Search Outcomes: Regression Discontinuity Estimates from Germany," IAB Discussion Paper 2010,4 (Institut für Arbeitsmarkt-und Berufsforschung, 2010), http://hdl.handle.net/10419/32764.

15. Bruce D. Meyer, "Unemployment and Workers' Compensation Programmes: Rationale, Design, Labour Supply and Income Support," *Fiscal Studies*, vol. 23, no. 1 (March 2002), pp. 1–49, http://onlinelibrary.wiley.com/doi/10.1111/j.1475-5890.2002.tb00053.x/abstract.

16. See Lawrence F. Katz and Bruce D. Meyer, "The Impact of the Potential Duration of Unemployment Benefits on the Duration of Unemployment," *Journal of Public Economics*, vol. 41, no. 1 (February 1990), pp. 45–72, www.sciencedirect.com/science/journal/00472727/41/1. For more recent evidence, see David Card and Phillip B. Levine, "Extended Benefits and the Duration of UI Spells: Evidence from the New Jersey Extended Benefit Program," *Journal of Public Economics*, vol. 78, nos. 1–2 (October 2000), pp. 107–138, www.sciencedirect.com/science/journal/00472727/78/1-2.

about 40 percent of that one-week increase was the result of a diminished incentive to take a job because of the "tax" induced by the reduction in benefits that result from increased earnings; the remaining 60 percent of that increase arose because unemployment insurance provides recipients with cash so that they feel less immediate pressure to take the first job they are offered.[17]

Differences When Unemployment Is High. The effects of UI benefits on the incentives that recipients have to search for and accept a job offer are different when unemployment is high. On the one hand, with fewer job openings, a job search is less likely to quickly result in employment, and so UI-induced reductions in the intensity of that search may matter less. On the other hand, UI benefits tend to replace a larger portion of prospective earnings when unemployment is high, because recipients' benefits are based on pay at their former job and not on the lower-paying jobs available in a recession or the early part of a recovery.[18] Thus, the UI-induced reduction in the net gain from returning to work may be bigger and of greater consequence in such periods.[19] Empirical assessments suggest that the recent extensions of benefits have lengthened spells of unemployment among UI recipients but that the effect of such extensions has been smaller than had been observed when the unemployment rate was lower.[20]

Potentially offsetting the disincentive effect that unemployment insurance has on recipients' reemployment is a resulting positive effect on the employment prospects of workers who are unemployed but are not eligible for UI benefits, such as people looking for their first job or reentering the labor force. In particular, to the extent that UI recipients are slower to accept available jobs, nonrecipients are more likely to receive a job offer. That positive effect tends to be larger when job openings are scarce, as they have been since the recent recession began.[21]

Effects of UI Taxes on Decisions About Employment

UI payroll taxes—which provide all of the funding for UI benefits under normal circumstances and have been supplemented by resources from general revenues in recent years—also change firms' and workers' decisions about employment.

Because firms' payroll taxes do not cover the full cost of UI benefits to the workers they lay off, unemployment insurance subsidizes both the hiring and the laying off of workers. High-layoff firms pay higher UI taxes because of experience rating, but those taxes are not enough, on average, to cover the higher costs those firms impose on the UI system.[22] As a result, firms with few layoffs provide implicit subsidies to firms with many layoffs. For example, older, established firms in service industries, which tend to have few layoffs, subsidize smaller, newer

17. See Raj Chetty, "Moral Hazard Versus Liquidity and Optimal Unemployment Insurance," *Journal of Political Economy*, vol. 116, no. 2 (April 2008), pp. 173–234, www.jstor.org/stable/10.1086/529035.

18. For a related discussion, see Steven J. Davis and Till Von Wachter, "Recessions and the Costs of Job Loss," *Brookings Papers on Economic Activity*, no. 1 (Fall 2011), pp. 1–55, www.brookings.edu/~/media/projects/bpea/fall%202011/2011b_bpea_davis.pdf.

19. Lars Ljunqvist and Thomas J. Sargent, "The European Unemployment Dilemma," *Journal of Political Economy*, vol. 106, no. 3 (June 1998), pp. 514–550, www.jstor.org/stable/10.1086/250020.

20. See, for example, Henry S. Farber and Robert Valletta, *Extended Unemployment Insurance and Unemployment Duration in the Great Recession: The U.S. Experience* (draft, June 24, 2011), www.frbsf.org/economics/economists/rvalletta/uiext.pdf (cited with permission from the authors); and Jesse Rothstein, "Unemployment Insurance and Job Search in the Great Recession," *Brookings Papers on Economic Activity*, no. 1 (Fall 2011), pp. 143–205, www.brookings.edu/about/projects/bpea/past-editions. Other economists have pointed to UI extensions, along with increased receipt of benefits from the Supplemental Nutrition Assistance Program (formerly known as the Food Stamp program) and other changes to means-tested programs, as a significant cause of sustained high unemployment during and following the recession. See, for example, Casey B. Mulligan, *Do Welfare Policies Matter for Labor Market Aggregates? Quantifying Safety Net Work Incentives Since 2007*, Working Paper 18088 (National Bureau of Economic Research, May 2012), www.nber.org/papers/w18088.

21. See Kory Kroft and Matthew J. Notowidigdo, "Should Unemployment Insurance Vary with the Unemployment Rate? Theory and Evidence" (draft, December 2011), http://faculty.chicagobooth.edu/matthew.notowidigdo; and Camille Landais, Pascal Michaillat, and Emmanuel Saez, *Optimal Unemployment Insurance Over the Business Cycle*, Working Paper 16526 (National Bureau of Economic Research, November 2010), www.nber.org/papers/w16526.

22. See Patricia M. Anderson and Bruce D. Meyer, "Unemployment Insurance in the United States: Layoff Incentives and Cross Subsidies," *Journal of Labor Economics*, vol. 11, no. 1, pt. 2 (January 1993), pp. S70–S95, www.jstor.org/stable/2535168.

firms in industries like construction, which tend to lay workers off more frequently.[23] Although levied as a payroll tax on employers, the portion of the cost of UI taxes that does not vary among firms within a local labor market is ultimately paid by workers in the form of reduced wages. Employment and workers' earnings therefore are probably higher in high-layoff industries, and lower in low-layoff industries, than they would be in the absence of unemployment insurance.

However, because experience rating means that high-layoff firms pay higher taxes to cover the costs they impose on the UI system—thereby mitigating some of the problems just discussed—the system provides slightly less insurance to firms and workers than it would if the funding for unemployment insurance came from sources other than payroll taxes. That insurance is provided against unexpected deterioration in business conditions, such as weak economywide demand for goods or increased prices of key inputs to production. Rather than spreading such risks more broadly by raising funds for unemployment insurance from general revenues, firms effectively repay the UI system for a portion of the benefits paid to workers whom they lay off. Those repayments take the form of higher subsequent UI taxes that, when passed through to the employees who remain with the firm, reduce wages—which slightly reduces the total amount of insurance provided by the UI system.

Some analysts also have expressed concern that because payroll taxes are linked to a firm's record of layoffs, businesses might seek to avoid paying higher taxes by misrepresenting layoffs in one of two ways: Firms might claim to have fired employees for cause or might assert that employees had left voluntarily.[24] In part because of such concerns, most European countries do not have experience rating as a feature of their UI tax system.[25] However, the UI-based incentive to misrepresent layoffs

as firings may be counteracted by an incentive created by the legal system to misrepresent firings as layoffs. Specifically, some research suggests that firms, in an effort to avoid being sued by employees upset about being fired, wait until periods of slack demand to lay off low-performing workers whom they would otherwise have fired earlier.[26]

Effects of the UI System as an Automatic Economic Stabilizer

Automatic economic stabilizers decrease government revenues and increase government expenditures in periods of weak economic activity without requiring new government action. They also reduce spending and boost revenues when economic activity is strong. The structure of taxes and benefits under the unemployment insurance system makes that system a prototypical automatic stabilizer.

Weak demand for goods and services during the recent recession and slow recovery has reduced output and employment, in CBO's view. Under those conditions, automatic stabilizers increase demand for goods and services by households, businesses, and governments and thereby increase overall output and employment.[27] UI benefits are particularly effective in that stabilizing role because they are directed toward families who, because of their changed employment circumstances, probably spend a large fraction of the benefits they receive.[28]

23. See Robert H. Topel, "On Layoffs and Unemployment Insurance," *American Economic Review*, vol. 73, no. 4 (September 1983), pp. 541–559, www.jstor.org/stable/10.2307/i331506; and Patricia M. Anderson and Bruce D. Meyer, "Unemployment Insurance in the United States: Layoff Incentives and Cross Subsidies," *Journal of Labor Economics*, vol. 11, no.1, pt. 2 (January 1993), pp. S70–S95, www.jstor.org/stable/2535168.

24. See Jerry L. Mashaw, *Unemployment Compensation: Continuity, Change, and the Prospects for Reform*, Faculty Scholarship Series, Paper 1187 (1996), http://digitalcommons.law.yale.edu/fss_papers/1187.

25. Julia Fath and Clemens Fuest, "Temporary Layoffs and Unemployment Insurance: Is Experience Rating Desirable?" *German Economic Review*, vol. 6, no. 4 (November 2005), pp. 471–483, http://onlinelibrary.wiley.com/doi/10.1111/j.1468-0475.2005.00142.x/abstract.

26. See, for example, Paul Oyer and Scott Schaefer, "Layoffs and Litigation," *Rand Journal of Economics*, vol. 31, no. 2 (Summer 2000), pp. 345–358, www.rje.org/archive.html.

27. For estimates of the magnitude of automatic stabilizers in the federal budget, see Congressional Budget Office, *The Budget and Economic Outlook: Fiscal Years 2012 to 2022* (January 2012), Appendix C, www.cbo.gov/publication/42905. For an analysis of the slow recovery, see Congressional Budget Office, *What Accounts for the Slow Growth of the Economy After the Recession?* (November 2012), www.cbo.gov/publication/43707.

28. For additional discussion, see the testimony of Douglas W. Elmendorf, Director, Congressional Budget Office, before the Senate Committee on the Budget, *Policies for Increasing Economic Growth and Employment in 2012 and 2013* (November 15, 2011), www.cbo.gov/publication/42717.

In CBO's assessment, the increase in the amount of UI benefits during the past several years—including the automatic increase in total benefits that would have occurred under previous law and the additional increase in benefits that was caused by changes in law—has raised consumer spending, output, and employment relative to what they otherwise would have been. Specifically, CBO concludes that, given the economic conditions that have prevailed, the positive impact of the additional UI benefits on the demand for goods and services—and thus on economic activity—has been significantly larger than the net impact on economic activity of the various other ways in which the increase in UI benefits has affected the economy (including greater incentives to search for a job and reduced incentives to accept a job offer).

As the economy improves, total UI benefits will automatically fall, and total UI taxes will automatically rise. That evolution will help stabilize economic activity in the future.

Policy Options for the Short Term

Unemployment has been at historically high levels since the recession began in late 2007 and has been slow to fall even though the recession officially ended in 2009. The creation of the EUC program and the other modifications to UI policy since 2008 reflect policymakers' concerns about the economic circumstances of people who have lost their job and have not taken a new one. Under current law, at the end of December 2012 the UI system will revert to the policies that were in place before the recession. As a result, eligibility for UI benefits will contract sharply, and federal spending for those benefits will decline sharply as well.

Policymakers could choose to continue offering additional weeks of UI benefits—for example, to keep some or all of the current policies that have been adopted in recent years in place for up to one additional year. Doing so would impose a budgetary cost on the federal government. CBO expects that such an extension also would increase output (gross domestic product, or GDP) and employment in the short term relative to what would otherwise occur. Using evidence from empirical studies and econometric models, CBO has estimated the impact of offering additional weeks of benefits on output and employment. In CBO's view, the various effects of extending additional unemployment benefits *apart from* the effects on the overall demand for goods and services

would, on balance, make little difference to overall output or the number of people employed under the weak economic conditions that the agency projects for the next few years. Accordingly, CBO's estimates of the impact of additional weeks of unemployment insurance on output and employment include only the effects of boosting demand for goods and services—using low and high estimates to encompass, in CBO's judgment, most economists' views about those effects.

Extending unemployment benefits for one year in either the EUC or the EB program would boost GDP in 2013 by $1.10 for every dollar of budgetary cost in that year, CBO estimates. That figure represents CBO's central estimate, which corresponds to the assumption that the values that describe key parameters of economic behavior (in particular, the extent to which lower federal taxes and higher federal spending boost aggregate demand in the short term) equal the midpoints of the ranges used by CBO.[29] The full ranges that CBO uses for those parameters suggest that if unemployment benefits were extended, then GDP could be between $0.40 and $1.80 higher per dollar of budgetary cost.

Regarding employment, CBO estimates that extending UI benefits for one year would add about 6 years of full-time-equivalent employment (FTE-years—that is, 40 hours of employment per week for one year) in 2013

---

29. For a discussion of CBO's approach to analyzing the short-term effects of fiscal policy, see Felix Reichling and Charles Whalen, *Assessing the Short-Term Effects on Output of Changes in Federal Fiscal Policies*, Congressional Budget Office Working Paper 2012-08 (May 2012), www.cbo.gov/publication/43278. CBO has previously analyzed the effects of increasing aid to the unemployed; see, for example, the testimony of Douglas W. Elmendorf, Director, Congressional Budget Office, before the Senate Committee on the Budget, *Policies for Increasing Economic Growth and Employment in 2012 and 2013* (November 15, 2011), pp. 26–27, www.cbo.gov/publication/42717. In the current report, CBO has refined some aspects of its analytic approach and its presentation of results. For example, CBO now estimates that changes in GDP affect employment more gradually than the agency estimated previously. That change implies that generating a given increase in employment in the first year of a policy requires a larger increase in GDP. In addition, CBO now presents the effects of policies on nominal GDP per dollar of budgetary cost, whereas the previous analysis presented the effects on real (inflation-adjusted) GDP measured with 2008 prices; that change in presentation (which better matches the effect on GDP to the budgetary cost of a policy, measured in nominal dollars) has slightly increased the effects on output per dollar of budgetary cost presented in this report but leaves the effects on employment unchanged.

Table 1.

Policy Options for Changing the Unemployment Insurance System in the Short Term and Their Costs

Option	Budgetary Cost
Option 1: Fully Extend the Emergency Employment Compensation (EUC) Program and Temporary Provisions of the Extended Benefits (EB) Program for One Year	$30 billion
Option 2: Partially Extend the EUC Program for One Year (Allow unemployment insurance recipients to continue to claim Tier I benefits but allow all other expiring provisions to lapse.)	$14 billion
Option 3: Allow Unemployment Insurance Recipients to Finish Receiving the Tier of EUC Benefits for Which They Will Qualify at the End of December 2012, Up to 14 Additional Weeks (Allow all other expiring provisions to lapse.)	$4 billion
Option 4: Extend Temporary Provisions of the EB Program for One Year	$3 billion
Option 5: Delay States' Schedules for Repaying the Unemployment Trust Fund for One Year	$3 billion in 2013, roughly offset by higher revenues in subsequent years

Source:　Congressional Budget Office.

Notes:　Unemployment insurance benefits are taxable under the federal income tax. According to standard Congressional scorekeeping practices, however, cost estimates of proposed legislation that would increase or decrease unemployment insurance benefits (or other taxable federal spending) do not take into account any resulting increases or decreases in federal tax revenues.

　　　　Tier I benefits are available in all states, regardless of the state's unemployment rate, and provide up to 14 additional weeks of benefits.

per million dollars of budgetary cost. Under alternative assumptions about economic behavior, that amount ranges from 2 to 10 FTE-years.

In contrast, CBO's estimates of the effect of providing additional UI benefits on the unemployment rate include both negative and positive values. On the one hand, the increase in employment would reduce the number of people without a job. On the other hand, to remain eligible for unemployment benefits, more people without a job would stay in the labor force and be counted as unemployed after their receipt of regular benefits ended. According to CBO's central estimate, extending UI benefits would cause an average of three additional people to be counted as unemployed during 2013 per million dollars of budgetary cost. According to CBO's estimate that incorporates a smaller effect on demand for goods and services (corresponding to 2 FTE-years) and a larger effect on people staying in the labor force, extending UI benefits would result in eight more people being counted as unemployed per million dollars of budgetary cost. Conversely, according to the agency's estimate that incorporates a larger effect on demand (corresponding to 10 FTE-years) and a smaller effect on people staying in

the labor force, extending UI benefits would result in two fewer people being counted as unemployed per million dollars of budgetary cost.

In this study, CBO examines five policy options and assesses their effects on the federal budget (see Table 1). Four options would extend some or all of the temporary UI provisions through the end of December 2013. In general, options that extend more of the temporary provisions would provide more benefits to laid-off workers and produce a larger increase in total output and employment, but they would also have a greater budgetary cost. The fifth option would change the schedule on which states repay amounts borrowed from the UI trust fund.

Current Law
Under current law, following the provisions of the Middle Class Tax Relief and Job Creation Act of 2012, four tiers of Emergency Unemployment Compensation benefits are available to unemployed workers from September 2, 2012, through the end of December 2012. Each successive tier of benefits adds to the benefits provided for the lower tiers, up to a maximum of

47 additional weeks (that is, 47 weeks of benefits beyond those provided by a state's regular UI program).[30]

■ Tier I benefits are available in all states, regardless of the state's unemployment rate (up to 14 additional weeks).

■ Tier II benefits are available in states whose unemployment rate is 6 percent or higher (up to 14 additional weeks).

■ Tier III benefits are available in states whose unemployment rate is 7 percent or higher (up to 9 additional weeks).

■ Tier IV benefits are available in states whose unemployment rate is 9 percent or higher (up to 10 additional weeks).

In September 2012, the number of states paying at least 50 new claims in those tiers was 50, 36, 28, and 12, respectively.[31]

Under current law, the extended benefits program will change in two ways in January 2013. First, the share of costs for that program paid by the federal government will revert from 100 percent to 50 percent (the share in effect before February 2009). Second, the temporary provisions allowing states to use a longer period to measure changes in their unemployment rate (that is, to use an extended look-back period) to determine eligibility for the program are also scheduled to end. Although workers in 41 of the 50 states have received extended benefits within the past five years, only one state (New York) was paying such benefits as of November 2012.

According to CBO's baseline projections, which generally follow current law, the unemployment rate will increase from 8.1 percent in the third quarter of 2012 to 9.1 percent in the fourth quarter of 2013. The reason for that

jump is that significant tax hikes and spending cuts scheduled to occur under current law in 2013 will reduce economic activity and increase unemployment for the next few years. As a result of that higher unemployment, CBO projects that the number of new UI recipients will be higher in 2013 than in 2012.[32] In addition, some states that are currently not eligible to participate in the EB program (because their unemployment rate is not sufficiently high) will probably become eligible—in some cases, regaining eligibility that had previously lapsed—as unemployment in those states goes up. In CBO's baseline projections, spending for regular and extended benefits totals about $49 billion in fiscal year 2013.

Option 1. Fully Extend the EUC Program and Temporary Provisions of the EB Program for One Year

Option 1 would extend all four tiers of the current EUC program through December 2013. In addition, the federal government would continue to pay the full cost of the EB program, and the provisions used to determine states' eligibility for that program (specifically, the three-year look-back period used to determine any increase in the unemployment rate) would continue through the end of 2013. CBO estimates that this option would cost the federal government roughly $30 billion.

CBO projects that extending benefits in this way would increase inflation-adjusted GDP by 0.2 percent (by 0.1 percent to 0.5 percent under CBO's full range of assumptions) and increase full-time-equivalent employment by 0.3 million (with a range from 0.1 million to 0.5 million) in the fourth quarter of 2013.[33] (The overall effects for the fourth quarter of 2013 are not equal to the

---

30. Benefits for some of those tiers are available for fewer weeks under current law than was the case in 2010 or 2011, when benefits were available for up to 53 additional weeks, and the state criteria for eligibility for different tiers of benefits have become more difficult to meet.

31. State counts are CBO estimates based on data from Department of Labor, "Emergency Unemployment Compensation 2008 (EUC2008) and Federal-State Extended Benefit (EB) Summary Data for State Programs," http://workforcesecurity.doleta.gov/unemploy/euc.asp. See "EUC Aggregate Program Activity," Data from July 2008 – Present.

32. Congressional Budget Office, *An Update to the Budget and Economic Outlook: Fiscal Years 2012 to 2022* (August 2012), www.cbo.gov/publication/43539.

33. This option is one component of the policy to "extend the reduction in employees' portion of the payroll tax and extend emergency unemployment benefits" that CBO previously analyzed. See Congressional Budget Office, *Economic Effects of Policies Contributing to Fiscal Tightening in 2013* (November 2012), p. 11, www.cbo.gov/publication/43694. The effect per dollar of budgetary cost of the UI extension alone is greater than the effect when such an extension is combined with a payroll tax reduction. The reason is that recipients would spend a larger portion of the additional UI benefits than of the tax savings, CBO estimates. However, the budgetary cost of the UI extension would be about one-quarter of the budgetary cost of a reduction of 2 percentage points in the payroll tax, so the UI extension is a relatively smaller part of the overall policy that CBO estimated previously.

corresponding effects per dollar multiplied by the budgetary cost reported above because of differences in the time periods analyzed.) The other options analyzed in this report would have smaller overall macroeconomic effects; because of their small size, CBO could not reliably quantify those effects.

Option 2. Partially Extend the EUC Program for One Year

This option would continue only the Tier I benefits of the EUC program through 2013 (Tier I provides up to 14 weeks of benefits once a UI recipient has exhausted benefits from the state's regular UI program). As under current law, the other three tiers would lapse at the end of 2012, and so would the EB program's temporary provisions of full federal funding and longer look-back period. Tier I accounts for a disproportionate share of the EUC program's total cost because states are eligible for benefits regardless of their unemployment rate. CBO estimates that this option would cost about $14 billion.

Option 3. Allow UI Recipients to Finish Receiving the Tier of EUC Benefits for Which They Will Qualify at the End of December 2012, Up to 14 Additional Weeks

Under current law, EUC benefits are scheduled to come to a "hard stop" in the first week of January, and no further payments will be made after that. Option 3 would allow UI recipients to finish the tier of EUC benefits that they are receiving at the end of December 2012, but it would not allow unemployed workers to initiate EUC benefits or to start a new tier of benefits. Some UI recipients would continue receiving benefits into April 2013 under this option, but EUC expenditures would quickly phase out as recipients completed their benefit tiers. This option would cost approximately $4 billion.

Option 4. Extend Temporary Provisions of the EB Program for One Year

Option 4 would maintain full federal funding and the current three-year look-back provisions of the EB program through December 2013 but would allow the EUC program to lapse at the end of 2012 as currently scheduled. Very few states will be eligible to provide extended benefits in 2013, CBO projects, because they will no longer meet the requirement that their unemployment rate be increasing relative to what it was three years ago, even though the number of unemployed people in the states may continue to be high. This option would cost approximately $3 billion.

Option 5. Delay States' Schedules for Repaying the Unemployment Trust Fund for One Year

Under current law, states that owe money to the UI trust fund must begin repaying that debt or have their FUTA taxes increased. That policy caused few problems in the past because when such balances were incurred during previous recessions, fairly rapid recoveries generated increases in UI revenues and decreases in UI benefits that allowed states to quickly pay off those balances. But states are currently required to raise UI payroll taxes while their labor markets are still weak, which may further impede growth in employment. Providing a one-year "holiday" from higher FUTA taxes would allow states to make repayments in 2014 and beyond, when labor markets will probably be stronger and higher taxes will have a smaller effect on employment. CBO estimates that this option would reduce federal revenues by $3 billion in 2013 but that the revenue loss would be roughly offset by increases in federal and state UI taxes in future years.

Policy Approaches for the Longer Term

CBO also considered a wide range of approaches for changing the structure of the UI system for the longer term (see Table 2). In its current form, the UI system raises funds via state and federal payroll taxes and allows states considerable leeway in deciding how to structure benefits so long as the benefits are paid to eligible unemployed workers in a timely fashion. The three sets of approaches assessed here would:

■ Restructure benefits to encourage employment,

■ Change the mix of federal and state roles, and

■ Change the distribution of resources within the UI system.

Because the budgetary effects of those approaches would depend on their specific design, CBO did not estimate their impact on the federal budget. Indeed, depending on how the approaches were implemented, they could increase or decrease the budgetary cost of the UI system for federal and state governments. Many of the approaches could be combined with one another, and they do not encompass all potential changes to the UI system. Many other changes are also possible.

Restructuring Benefits to Encourage Employment

Policymakers seeking to encourage employment could modify the form of benefits that laid-off workers receive.

Table 2.

Policy Approaches for Changing the Unemployment Insurance System Over the Longer Term

Approach	Description
Restructuring Benefits to Encourage Employment	
Providing Reemployment Bonuses	Make laid-off workers eligible to receive a lump-sum payment if they are reemployed within a specified period.
Establishing Personal Reemployment Accounts	Make laid-off workers who are at risk of remaining unemployed for more than 26 weeks eligible to receive funds in a dedicated account that they can use to pay for career training or reemployment bonuses.
Establishing Unemployment Insurance Savings Accounts	Require workers to save a fixed percentage of their before-tax income in an account and allow eligible unemployed workers to withdraw amounts equal to current UI benefits. (At retirement, convert any positive account balances to an individual retirement account and forgive any negative balances.)
Expanding the Use of Short-Time Compensation	Encourage states to provide unemployment benefits to workers who have their hours reduced by their employer instead of being laid off.
Changing the Mix of Federal and State Roles	
Giving States More Predictability in Funding and More Flexibility in Implementing Their UI Program	Tie federal funding to formulas based on economic conditions or other factors and give states more latitude to determine how to use the funds.
Making State Programs More Uniform	Require states to set benefits and taxes within a narrower range than is currently allowed.
Changing the Distribution of Resources Within the Unemployment Insurance System	
Changing the Limit on Taxable Earnings	Increase the amount of an employee's annual earnings that is subject to the state and federal taxes that fund unemployment insurance. (That approach could be coupled with lower tax rates to keep unchanged the amount of tax revenue that is collected.)
Changing the Amount of Weekly Unemployment Insurance Benefits	Increase the share of income that is replaced by unemployment insurance benefits or increase the cap on income that can be replaced by such insurance.
Providing Earnings Insurance	Give eligible laid-off workers who are reemployed at a job paying less than their prior job a portion of the difference between their original earnings and new earnings.

Source: Congressional Budget Office.

For example, the UI system could be modified to provide reemployment bonuses, establish personal reemployment accounts, establish unemployment insurance savings accounts, or encourage the use of short-time compensation.

Providing Reemployment Bonuses. To provide incentives for UI recipients to quickly return to work, the federal government could establish a system of reemployment bonuses—one-time payments to UI recipients who

find work within a specified period after losing their job. The potential advantages of such a policy are that, by paying UI recipients to return to work, bonuses could reduce joblessness and potentially reduce UI spending. Reemployment bonuses might be particularly effective at reducing the number of long spells of unemployment because unemployed workers would receive less money if they were still unemployed after the period of eligibility for the bonus ended. That effect may be more important now than in the past, given that long-term unemployment has become more common in the past decade, particularly since the recent recession began.

Whether this approach would reduce or increase UI spending is unclear, however. Offering reemployment bonuses to all UI recipients, regardless of how long they have been unemployed, might induce more eligible people to apply for benefits and would therefore substantially add to the program's cost, all else being equal. In addition, if bonuses were available to all UI recipients, bonuses might end up being provided to many people who would have taken a job quickly even without the bonus. If, instead, bonuses were offered only to people who have been unemployed for a long time—say, 15 or 20 weeks—then such bonuses might induce the newly jobless to stay unemployed until they qualified for bonus payments. Experiments in the 1980s and 1990s yielded mixed results about whether such bonuses reduced the number of weeks that laid-off workers received UI benefits.[34]

A closely related policy—the use of employment retention bonuses—has been used with success in the United Kingdom. Under the U.K. Employment Retention and Advancement program, the long-term unemployed who found a job received a retention bonus of £400 (approximately $600) every four months (for up to two years) if they continued working for at least 30 hours a week and for 13 weeks out of every 17.[35] Participants also received employment counseling, tuition assistance, and additional bonuses if they underwent training. The participants had significantly higher employment rates and earnings over the five-year study period than did long-term unemployed workers who did not participate. Furthermore, the cost to the government of providing such bonuses was less than the cost of providing standard employment assistance and services.

Establishing Personal Reemployment Accounts. The federal government could provide incentives for states to set up personal reemployment accounts (PRAs) that UI recipients would use to fund career training or reemployment bonuses. Some states currently have PRAs, which are self-managed accounts that are typically offered to people projected to be at risk of remaining unemployed for more than 26 weeks. Like the reemployment bonuses discussed above, PRAs encourage UI recipients to quickly return to work and thus receive the bonus. Also, PRAs eliminate any incentive for UI recipients to prolong unemployment because, unlike regular UI benefits, the cumulative value of the PRA benefits does not rise with weeks of joblessness. PRAs share some of the disadvantages of reemployment bonuses, however; by making unemployment insurance more appealing, the policy may increase the number of people receiving UI benefits and the cost of the program. In addition, states would incur additional administrative costs to teach recipients how to use the accounts.

In a demonstration project conducted in 2004, eight states provided $3,000 to selected UI recipients to use as a reemployment bonus or to purchase reemployment services.[36] In a related initiative in 2006, eight states provided $3,000 per year for two years to fund PRAs for UI recipients to pursue training.[37] The effects of those experiments on recipients were not evaluated directly, but the accounts established in the experiments were similar to individual training accounts that had been available earlier and were found to have little impact either on the amount of training received or on other outcomes when compared with the counseling services that states typically provided in One-Stop Career Centers.[38] The labor market was stronger during that demonstration than it is today, however, and such accounts might be more effec-

34. Bruce D. Meyer, "Lessons from the U.S. Unemployment Insurance Experiments," *Journal of Economic Literature*, vol. 33, no. 1 (March 1995), pp. 91–131, www.jstor.org/stable/2728911?seq=4.

35. See Richard Hendra and others, *Breaking the Low-Pay, No-Pay Cycle: Final Evidence from the U.K. Employment Retention and Advancement (ERA) Demonstration,* Research Report 765 (United Kingdom Department for Work and Pensions, August 2011), http://research.dwp.gov.uk/asd/asd5/report_abstracts/rr_abstracts/rra_765.asp.

36. See Gretchen Kirby and others, *Responses to Personal Reemployment Accounts (PRAs): Findings from the Demonstration States* (report submitted by Mathematica Policy Research, Inc., to the Department of Labor, June 2008), www.mathematica-mpr.com/labor/pra.asp.

37. See Jeffrey Salzman and others, *Evaluation of the Career Advancement Accounts Demonstration Project: An Implementation Study* (interim report submitted by Social Policy Research Associates to the Department of Labor, November 2010), http://wdr.doleta.gov/research/FullText_Documents/ETAOP_2011-17.pdf.

38. Sheena McConnell and others, *Managing Customers' Training Choices: Findings from the Individual Training Account Experiment* (final report submitted by Mathematica Policy Research, Inc., to the Department of Labor, December 2006), www.mathematica-mpr.com/labor/ita.asp.

tive under the weak labor market conditions projected for the next few years.

The federal government could provide additional waivers from the Social Security Act of 1935—the original enabling legislation for unemployment insurance—for states to experiment further with PRAs. Policymakers could also provide financial incentives to states to adopt and fund PRA programs, either through block grants or through matching grants. Those financial incentives could encourage states to use PRAs more widely than they otherwise would.

Establishing Unemployment Insurance Savings Accounts. An alternative to unemployment insurance is for workers to save money during periods of steady work to build a "rainy-day fund" in preparation for potential layoffs— a strategy commonly referred to as self-insurance—and to make cash available by facilitating borrowing after workers are laid off.

Unemployment insurance savings accounts provide some of the insurance and liquidity benefits of unemployment insurance but retain some of the incentives to work that self-insurance would provide. Under such a policy, workers would be required to deposit a fixed percentage of their before-tax earnings into their account. Those funds would earn interest and be available for weekly withdrawals by workers eligible for unemployment benefits. Eligible workers could borrow from their account, up to a limit, if their prior savings did not cover their withdrawals, and workers would pay off those debts through deposits they make once reemployed. An account that had a positive balance when the worker retired would be converted to an individual retirement account, and negative balances would be forgiven. Simulations suggest that if the contribution rate was 4 percent, a small fraction of workers would end their career with a negative account balance.[39] Similar accounts have been used to replace or supplement traditional UI systems in many Latin American countries.[40] To implement such accounts on a trial basis, the federal government could provide states with waivers from the Social Security Act.

The accounts would eliminate most of the adverse effects that UI has on incentives to find a job, because workers who take a job do not lose UI benefits; instead, they are able to keep more funds in their account or do not have to pay back borrowing from their account later. Such accounts would also supply much of the financial liquidity that UI provides, thereby allowing UI recipients to avoid having to sell assets or take out a high-interest loan.

A disadvantage of the accounts is that they do not provide as much protection against loss of earnings as do regular UI benefits. Workers themselves, not the government, provide that protection through their own saving and borrowing, which eliminates some of UI's positive effect on workers' willingness to take a high-risk/high-reward job, such as working for a new, small business. That disadvantage may be less important, however, if lawmakers view UI's primary function as providing financial liquidity rather than insurance.

Expanding the Use of Short-Time Compensation. Short-time compensation (STC) provides UI benefits to workers whose employers reduced their hours of work in lieu of laying them off. Because the traditional UI system provides benefits only for workers whose hours have been cut to zero, it creates an incentive for firms to reduce labor costs by laying off workers rather than by reducing the number of hours each employee works.[41] By providing UI benefits to people whose hours are cut, STC motivates firms to retain more workers at fewer hours per week, potentially reducing the number of layoffs and mitigating the effect of a recession on the unemployment rate. Some evidence indicates that European countries avoided some of the rise in unemployment that occurred

---

39. See Martin Feldstein and Daniel Altman, "Unemployment Insurance Savings Accounts," in James M. Poterba, ed., *Tax Policy and the Economy*, vol. 21 (MIT Press, 2007), pp. 35–64, www.nber.org/chapters/c0046.

40. See Ana M. Ferrer and W. Craig Riddell, *Unemployment Insurance Savings Accounts in Latin America: Overview and Assessment*, SP Discussion Paper 0910, Social Protection & Labor (World Bank, June 2009), http://siteresources.worldbank.org/SOCIALPROTECTION/Resources/SP-Discussion-papers/Labor-Market-DP/0910.pdf.

41. Those incentives are easiest to see in firms that have frequent short-term fluctuations in the amount of work needed, such as construction firms. For example, a firm that always needs 50 percent fewer labor hours in winter can cut each worker's hours by half each winter and, collectively, the workers would not receive UI benefits in the absence of short-time compensation. Alternatively, the firm can fully lay off half its workers in winter and keep the other half working full-time. As a group, the firm's workers share the same amount of work and earnings but now also receive UI benefits.

in the United States during and after the recent recession because they made greater use of STC policies.[42]

Some potential advantages of STC programs—particularly in a recession, when firms are uncertain about demand for their services or products—are that firms and workers gain time to make adjustments while maintaining valuable knowledge and skills. For example, if a firm is not able to return to its previous level of full-time employment, natural attrition may make it possible to increase the hours of remaining employees over time, even if the total hours of work needed by the firm are permanently lower. For workers, the loss of wages resulting from working fewer hours is spread across a larger group of people rather than being concentrated on those who have been laid off. Furthermore, workers may use the time when they are not working to find a new job, avoiding some or all of the potential permanent wage losses associated with layoffs.

Although 20 states operated STC programs as part of their unemployment insurance in 2011, those programs are not widely used and represent only about 1 percent of overall disbursements in the UI system.[43] Several factors may account for that infrequent use. Employers that might participate in an STC program may be unaware it exists if it is not widely publicized by a state. Also, short-time work may be uneconomical for workers who have lengthy commutes or other fixed costs associated with employment. Finally, STC is currently designed as an alternative to *temporary* or seasonal layoffs—situations in which firms know they will be able to recall laid-off workers after a certain period. But short-term layoffs are

increasingly uncommon, in part because of the relative decline in employment in unionized and manufacturing firms, which have made greatest use of them in the past.

The Middle Class Tax Relief and Job Creation Act of 2012 provided temporary subsidies to qualified STC programs and allocated roughly $100 million to expand states' use of STC programs. Under that legislation, the benefit costs of qualified STC programs will be paid from federal sources for up to three years. In addition, each state has a designated allotment from which it can draw to implement new programs or improve existing ones. States are directed to use one-third of the allotted grant money to implement or improve a short-time compensation program and two-thirds to promote and enroll employers in the program. That grant money may help invigorate STC programs, but federal policymakers may want to take further steps to encourage states to make greater use of such programs. For example, policymakers could provide federal matching funds for STC benefits paid out beyond the three years provided for under current law.

Changing the Mix of Federal and State Roles

Policymakers could alter the mix of responsibilities of the federal government and state governments in the UI system either to provide more autonomy to states to tailor unemployment benefits to their own circumstances or to provide a more uniform national program. The UI system currently involves a complex combination of federal and state roles with regard to determining eligibility for UI benefits, the amounts of benefits, and the taxation to fund the benefits. On one hand, states would probably engage in more policy innovation if they had more predictable funding and more flexibility in implementing their UI program. For example, states could use such latitude to fund a broader set of UI benefits, to provide training to laid-off workers, or to provide more intensive assistance to people seeking work. On the other hand, greater uniformity of state UI programs would probably reduce the incentives that firms and individuals have to seek states that offer relatively low costs for doing business or relatively generous benefits, respectively. The impact of either sort of change on federal and state budgets would depend on how taxes and benefits were modified.

Giving States More Predictability in Funding and More Flexibility in Implementing Their UI Program. Policymakers could make federal funding for unemployment

---

42. See, for example, Pierre Cahuc and Stéphane Carcillo, *Is Short-Time Work a Good Method to Keep Unemployment Down?* IZA Discussion Paper 5430 (Institute for the Study of Labor, January 2011), www.iza.org/en/webcontent/publications/papers/viewAbstract?dp_id=5430; Michael C. Burda and Jennifer Hunt, "What Explains the German Labor Market Miracle in the Great Recession?" *Brookings Papers on Economic Activity* (Spring 2011), pp. 273–333, www.brookings.edu/about/projects/bpea/past-editions; and Tito Boeri and Herbert Bruecker, "Short-Time Work Benefits Revisited: Some Lessons from the Great Recession," *Economic Policy*, vol. 26, no. 68 (October 2011), pp. 697–765, http://onlinelibrary.wiley.com/doi/10.1111/j.1468-0327.2011.271.x/abstract.

43. Alison Shelton, *Compensated Work Sharing Arrangements (Short-Time Compensation) as an Alternative to Layoffs*, CRS Report for Congress R40689 (Congressional Research Service, February 15, 2011).

insurance more predictable. Although the federal government accounts for a small share of overall state and federal spending on unemployment insurance when unemployment is low, federal spending has typically soared during recent recessions. Some of that increased spending occurs automatically through the permanent cost-sharing features of the extended benefits program. In the recent recession, however, most of the increase in federal spending on unemployment insurance occurred through new policies such as emergency benefits, additional compensation, and the modifications to the extended benefits program.

Increases in federal funding during and after recessions could be made more formulaic by automatically tying more funding to state and national unemployment rates, for example, instead of relying on new policies. Tying funding to such formulas would make federal assistance to states more predictable when state governments' fiscal situations are typically under stress. However, policymakers may wish to tailor federal responses to particular circumstances rather than rely on formulas.

Policymakers also could give states wider autonomy in determining how states spend their unemployment insurance funds. States already have considerable freedom to set their own tax rates and benefit levels, but under this approach they could allocate some funds to job training or other activities designed to increase employment, such as those discussed above. If such experimentation was effective, other states could learn from the results and perhaps adopt similar approaches. The wider autonomy could be allowed on spending funded by state unemployment taxes, by federal disbursements, or by spending funded from either source.

Giving states more flexibility has some potential disadvantages, however. For example, the UI system might become a less effective automatic economic stabilizer in a recession if the funds states gave to unemployed workers were in a form less likely to be immediately spent—such as a reemployment bonus or a personal reemployment account.

Making State Programs More Uniform. Policymakers could make state UI programs more uniform than they are currently. For example, they could require that states' tax and benefit policies be within a narrower range than under current policy, or they could federalize the UI system by collecting taxes and administering benefits at the federal rather than at the state level. (In virtually all countries in Western Europe, UI policies are administered at the national level).[44]

The structure of unemployment insurance benefits and taxes differs considerably among states.[45] Those differences may influence employers' decisions about when and where to invest. Economic efficiency can be reduced when firms make fewer or less productive investments to avoid UI taxation. As a result, greater uniformity among states' UI systems would reduce the distortions of business decisions caused by differences in states' UI policies.

Greater uniformity would have disadvantages, however. To the extent that states' residents differ in their earnings, their likelihood of being laid off, or their household wealth, for example, they may prefer UI programs that differ from one another. To the extent that people choose to live in a state because of its policies (including UI policy), permitting differences between states allows people to "vote with their feet" and live in states that have the combination of policies that best suits their circumstances and preferences.[46]

Changing the Distribution of Resources Within the UI System

Policymakers could alter the way that income is redistributed within the UI system. For example, they could change the limit on taxable earnings, change the amount of weekly UI benefits, or establish wage insurance for workers. Depending on the precise nature of the changes made, those policies would either increase or decrease the share of unemployment insurance benefits provided to workers who have low earnings or, independently, the share of benefits provided to workers who have longer-term reductions in earnings.

44. Katherine Baicker, Claudia Goldin, and Lawrence F. Katz, "A Distinctive System: Origins and Impact of U.S. Unemployment Compensation," in Michael D. Bordo, Claudia Goldin, and Eugene N. White, eds., *The Defining Moment: The Great Depression and the American Economy in the Twentieth Century* (University of Chicago Press, 1998), pp. 227–264, www.nber.org/chapters/c6895.

45. See Department of Labor, "State Law Information" (August 16, 2012), http://workforcesecurity.doleta.gov/unemploy/statelaws.asp.

46. Charles M. Tiebout, "A Pure Theory of Local Expenditures," *Journal of Political Economy*, vol. 64, no. 5 (October 1956), pp. 416–424, www.jstor.org/stable/1826343.

Changing the Limit on Taxable Earnings. One approach to changing the amount of redistribution within the UI system would be to alter the limit on earnings that are subject to the federal unemployment tax. For instance, that limit could be increased, and the new amount could be indexed so that it would grow with changes in wages in the future (as the earnings limit for Social Security currently does). Such an increase would impose a larger tax burden on workers who earn relatively more and, if combined with a reduction in the tax rate so that the total amount of tax revenue was unchanged, would also reduce taxes for workers who earn relatively less. Because states are required to set their own limit on taxable earnings at least as high as that of the federal government, an increase in the federal limit also would increase the limit of many state UI payroll taxes—amplifying the distributional effects of the policy.

The limit on each individual's earnings at a firm that are taxable under FUTA has remained constant at $7,000 since 1983—a period over which median weekly earnings have more than doubled. An increase in the limit on taxable earnings would raise average tax rates on higher earners. For example, a worker who earns $7,000 pays an average FUTA tax rate of 0.6 percent ($42/$7,000), but a worker who earns $14,000 pays an average FUTA tax rate of 0.3 percent ($42/$14,000). If tax rates remained the same, raising the taxable wage base to $14,000 would equalize the average FUTA tax rates of those two workers at 0.6 percent.

Increasing the limit on earnings that are subject to the FUTA tax would reduce the disincentive for employers to hire part-time workers. The current limit tends to discourage firms from hiring part-time workers because the employer would pay a larger amount of FUTA tax for two people earning $7,000 than for one person earning $14,000. Because there is no tax on earnings above the limit, the tax has a larger effect on the number of workers than it does on the number of hours that people work once they have a job. Even so, the FUTA tax is a small portion of the total cost of employing most workers—a maximum tax of $42 per worker—so the effects of this disincentive are probably small.

Changing the Amount of Weekly UI Benefits. The federal government could increase the benefits available to workers in two ways: by requiring states to adopt a higher replacement rate for earnings or by increasing the cap on the amount of earnings that could be replaced by unemployment insurance. The average UI replacement rate—the ratio of benefits to a worker's earnings before being laid off—ranged from 44 percent to 47 percent between 1988 and 2007.[47] For UI recipients whose benefits are less than the maximum amount, the basic weekly benefit is equal to or slightly greater than 50 percent of prior earnings in most states. States then cap that benefit at a maximum weekly amount. Currently, UI benefit amounts and formulas vary significantly from state to state.

Raising only the base replacement rate would not alter the benefits of high earners, but it would increase the UI benefits of lower-earning workers who were laid off. Alternatively, leaving the base replacement rate as is but raising the cap on benefits would have no effect on the UI benefits of workers whose earnings were below the prior cap, but it would increase benefits for high earners who were previously receiving the maximum benefit amount.

Either approach would increase the *average* UI replacement rate and would increase the economic effects of unemployment insurance. In particular, higher replacement rates would provide workers with more insurance against the loss of earnings from a layoff, but they would also provide additional incentives for laid-off workers to remain on unemployment insurance as long as they are eligible.

Providing Earnings Insurance. Policymakers could choose to adopt earnings insurance (also referred to as wage insurance) to temporarily make up some of the earnings gap for laid-off workers reemployed at reduced pay rates. Proposals to do that vary in such crucial specifics as the percentage of the drop in earnings that insurance would replace, the length of time over which payments could be received, and whether the insurance was based on annual earnings or hourly wages. Nonetheless, a simple example illustrates the program. If a worker earning $50,000 per year was laid off and then took a new job paying $40,000 per year, a program that insured 50 percent of earnings would pay the worker an additional $5,000 per year—half the difference between the worker's former and current earnings. Those payments

---

47. Government Accountability Office, *Unemployment Insurance Trust Funds: Long-Standing State Financing Policies Have Increased Risk of Insolvency*, GAO-10-440 (April 2010), p. 22, www.gao.gov/products/GAO-10-440.

might continue, for example, for five years and also might be structured to diminish over the course of the payout.

An earnings insurance program already exists for workers age 50 or older under the Reemployment Trade Adjustment Assistance program, most recently authorized by the Trade Adjustment Assistance Extension Act of 2011 and set to expire at the end of 2013. Eligibility for the program is restricted to laid-off workers deemed to have lost their job for reasons related to international trade. With some exceptions, that program has replaced 50 percent of participants' lost earnings, up to a maximum payment of $10,000 over two years, and only for workers' whose new job pays less than $50,000 per year.[48]

Earnings insurance, either as a substitute for or as a complement to the current UI system, would have several effects. The primary effect would be to provide insurance payments tied more directly to the larger, longer-term financial consequences of losing a job that the current UI system does not address. Research indicates that the average earnings of laid-off workers are significantly lower for many years after a layoff, which implies that the UI system protects workers only to a limited extent from the adverse financial consequences of losing a job.[49] For example, one recent study found that average earnings six years after a layoff were about 15 percent lower than they were before the layoff.[50] Earnings insurance would protect workers against some of that loss and would be targeted toward workers with the largest long-term reductions in earnings.

In principle, earnings insurance also could provide an incentive for some laid-off workers to go back to work sooner than they otherwise would, because their earnings while reemployed would be higher than they would be without the earnings insurance—an effect similar to that of reemployment bonuses. A study of earnings insurance in Canada, however, found little effect on the length of time before laid-off workers found another job.[51] Such insurance might also induce some laid-off workers to take a job that was less demanding and lower paying because the insurance would make up some of the earnings shortfall relative to their earnings at their prior job. However, other research finds that neither hours worked nor earnings are very responsive to changes in tax rates or reductions in benefit rates for workers earning between $10,000 and $50,000—the earnings range of many potential recipients of earnings insurance.[52] In sum, such potential recipients are more likely to be reemployed (so as to receive insurance payments) but also are more likely to earn less than they might otherwise (because insurance payments increase the financial benefit of returning to work); however, the effects of both incentives would probably be small.

---

48. See Benjamin Collins, *Trade Adjustment Assistance for Workers*, CRS Report for Congress R42012 (Congressional Research Service, July 11, 2012).

49. For a discussion of the consequences of being laid off, see Congressional Budget Office, *Losing a Job During a Recession* (April 2010), http://www.cbo.gov/publication/21396.

50. Kenneth A. Couch and Dana W. Placzek, "Earnings Losses of Displaced Workers Revisited," *American Economic Review*, vol. 100, no. 1 (March 2010), pp. 572–589, www.aeaweb.org/articles.php?doi=10.1257/aer.100.1. See also Till von Wachter, Jae Song, and Joyce Manchester, "Long-Term Earnings Losses Due to Mass Layoffs During the1982 Recession: An Analysis Using U.S. Administrative Data from 1974 to 2004" (draft, Columbia University, April 2009; cited with permission from the author), www.columbia.edu/~vw2112/papers/mass_layoffs_1982.pdf.

51. Howard S. Bloom and others, "Testing a Financial Incentive to Promote Re-Employment Among Displaced Workers: The Canadian Earnings Supplement Project (ESP)," *Journal of Policy Analysis and Management*, vol. 20, no. 3 (Summer 2001), pp. 505–523, http://onlinelibrary.wiley.com/doi/10.1002/pam.1005/abstract.

52. See Jon Gruber and Emmanuel Saez, "The Elasticity of Taxable Income: Evidence and Implications," *Journal of Public Economics*, vol. 84, no. 1 (April 2002), pp. 1–32, www.sciencedirect.com/science/journal/00472727/84/1; and Nada Eissa and Hilary W. Hoynes, "Behavioral Responses to Taxes: Lessons from the EITC and Labor Supply," in James M. Poterba, ed., *Tax Policy and the Economy*, vol. 20 (2006), pp. 73–110, www.nber.org/chapters/c0063.

List of Tables and Figures

Tables

Figures